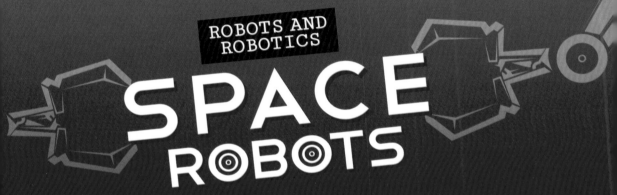

ROBOTS AND ROBOTICS

SPACE ROBOTS

RYAN NAGELHOUT

PowerKiDS
press™

New York

Published in 2017 by The Rosen Publishing Group, Inc.
29 East 21st Street, New York, NY 10010

First Edition

Editor: Caitie McAneney
Book Design: Reann Nye

Photo Credits: Cover, pp. 8, 9, 17, 18, 19 courtesy of NASA/JPL-Caltech; p. 4 kontur-vid/ Shutterstock.com; p. 5 NASA/Handout/Getty Images News/Getty Images; p. 6 Erich Auerbach/ Hulton Archive/Getty Images; p. 7 James Steidl/Shutterstock.com; p. 10 https://commons.wikimedia.org/ wiki/File:NASA_Mars_Rover.jpg; p. 12 https://commons.wikimedia.org/wiki/File:Curiosity_Self-Portrait_ at_%27Big_Sky%27_Drilling_Site.jpg; p. 13 https://commons.wikimedia.org/wiki/File:Mariner09.jpg; p. 14 https://commons.wikimedia.org/wiki/File:Huygens_probe_dsc03686.jpg; p. 15 https:// commons.wikimedia.org/wiki/File:Cassini_Saturn_Orbit_Insertion.jpg; p. 21 https://commons. wikimedia.org/wiki/File:Mars_Reconnaissance_Orbiter.jpg; p. 22 https://commons.wikimedia.org/wiki/ File:HST-SM4.jpeg; p. 24 https://commons.wikimedia.org/wiki/File:Robonaut_2_working.jpg; p. 25 Stocktrek Images/Getty Images; p. 26 https://en.wikipedia.org/wiki/File:STS-114_Steve_ Robinson_on_Canadarm2.jpg; p. 27 https://en.wikipedia.org/wiki/File:Dextrereallyhasnohead.jpg; p. 29 https://commons.wikimedia.org/wiki/File:Three_SPHERES_on_International_Space_Station.jpg; p. 30 courtesy of Joe Bibby/NASA Johnson Space Center/Flickr.com.

Library of Congress Cataloging-in-Publication Data

Names: Nagelhout, Ryan, author.
Title: Space robots / Ryan Nagelhout.
Description: New York : PowerKids Press, [2016] | Series: Robots and
  robotics | Includes index.
Identifiers: LCCN 2016012339 | ISBN 9781499421859 (pbk.) | ISBN 9781499421835 (library
bound) | ISBN 9781499421828 (6 pack)
Subjects: LCSH: Space robotics–Juvenile literature. | Space probes–Juvenile
  literature. | Robotics–Juvenile literature. | Outer
  space–Exploration–Juvenile literature.
Classification: LCC TL1097 .N34 2016 | DDC 629.43–dc23
LC record available at http://lccn.loc.gov/2016012339

Manufactured in the United States of America

CPSIA Compliance Information: Batch #BS16PK: For Further Information contact Rosen Publishing, New York, New York at 1-800-237-9932

CONTENTS

FIRST IN SPACE

Before scientists and engineers sent humans into space, they sent machines. The first artificial, or man-made, **satellite** to leave Earth was called *Sputnik*. Launched into orbit by the Soviet Union on October 4, 1957, the satellite was about the size of a beach ball. Since then, man-made technology has been used to explore space before people do for a number of reasons. It's safer, of course, but it also costs less because machines don't need oxygen to breathe or food to eat. That means they can travel farther away from Earth.

SPUTNIK

Many of the machines we put into space aren't designed to come back. You can't do the same thing with people!

Today, we have many kinds of robots in space. Some are traveling millions of miles away, exploring the outer reaches of our galaxy. Others help the people who live and work in space aboard the **International Space Station** (ISS). Let's learn more about space robots!

WHAT'S A SPACE ROBOT?

When you think of space robots, you might imagine people-shaped machines aboard advanced spaceships. While that might fit Czech author Karel Čapek's original definition of the word "robot," that's science fiction and not science. Most of the robots we've sent into space don't look like us but rather like cars, spaceships, or even just mechanical arms.

ROSSUM'S UNIVERSAL ROBOTS

Czech author Karel Čapek invented the word "robot" when he wrote a play called *R.U.R.: Rossum's Universal Robots*, which was published in 1920. In the play, a company makes humanlike machines that do work humans find dull or even dangerous, or unsafe. The word "robot" actually comes from the Czech word "robota," which means "forced labor." In a way, Čapek imagined what robots do today: the work we can't or don't want to do.

The robots that help astronauts in space today are far from the science-fiction robots we imagined in the past.

The newer definition of a robot is a mechanical tool that helps people perform tasks or completes tasks on its own. Space robots work with scientists and engineers to perform experiments and help astronauts take care of the ISS. Some robots even work on their own, exploring regions of space so far away that humans can't travel there. The robots send their findings—and some amazing photographs—back to Earth for scientists to study.

EARLY SPACE ROBOTS

The first robots in space were called probes. These
are spacecraft designed to leave Earth to study something
in space. *Mariner 2* completed the first successful robotic
study of another planet. The National Aeronautics and Space
Administration (NASA) launched this probe on August 27,
1962. *Mariner 2* flew by Venus on a
three-month mission. *Mariner 4* flew
by Mars in 1965 and became the first
probe to take a picture.

MARINER 2

How Did Mariner 2 Work?

Mariner 2 weighed 450 pounds (204 kg) and
carried six different scientific tools to study Venus's
temperature, magnetism, dust makeup, and more.
It had a two-way radio to send data back to Earth
and let scientists at the Jet **Propulsion** Lab in
Pasadena, California, track the probe's path through
space. It was powered by solar panels. *Mariner 2*
learned that Venus's surface is about 900 degrees
Fahrenheit (482.2 degrees Celsius) before it lost
contact with Earth on January 3, 1963.

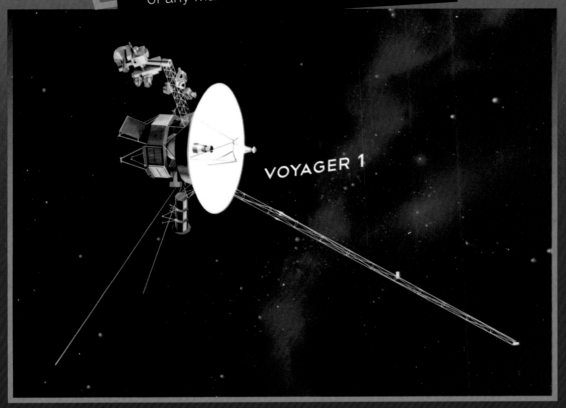

VOYAGER 1

The *Voyager 1* space probe was launched in 1977. In 2013, NASA announced that *Voyager 1* was the first man-made object to reach **interstellar** space. That means it left our solar system! Over time, scientists have designed probes with new tools with which to explore space in different ways.

ORBITERS, LANDERS, AND ROVERS

Today, the robots we use to study space fall into three basic groups: orbiters, landers, and rovers. Orbiters are robots designed to orbit, or travel around, an object such as a planet or moon.

Some spacecraft are designed to reach the surface of a planet, moon, or another body in space. These are called landers. A rover is a robot designed to reach the surface of a body in space and actually travel to certain places on its surface. Rovers collect samples, perform experiments, and take lots of photographs.

The space rovers *Spirit*, *Opportunity*, and *Curiosity* have traveled across many regions of Mars. They've made many observations about the planet's geography and conditions. Maybe humans will travel to Mars one day, but until then, space robots are the closest we've come.

THE HISTORY OF SPACE ROBOTS

OCTOBER 4, 1957
Sputnik 1 is the first spacecraft to orbit Earth.

SEPTEMBER 14, 1959
Luna 2 is the first spacecraft to reach the surface of the moon.

DECEMBER 14, 1962
Mariner 2 is the first spacecraft to reach another planet (Venus).

NOVEMBER 14, 1971
Mariner 9 becomes the first spacecraft to orbit another planet (Mars).

JULY 20, 1976
Viking 1 becomes the first spacecraft to land on Mars.

MAY 20, 1990
The Hubble Space Telescope takes its first photos in orbit around Earth.

JULY 5, 1997
Sojourner is the first rover to explore the surface of Mars.

FEBRUARY 14, 2000
The Near Earth Asteroid Rendezvous (NEAR) becomes the first spacecraft to orbit an asteroid (Eros).

AUGUST 6, 2012
Curiosity rover lands on Mars.

OCTOBER 2013
NASA reports Voyager 1 is the first man-made object to leave our solar system.

11

DIFFERENT ROBOTS, SAME PARTS

Though no two orbiters, rovers, or landers are alike, they do share the same basic parts. Most leave Earth carried by rockets, which use powerful fuel to propel the robot, or move it forward, beyond the pull of Earth's gravity and into space. Once they leave Earth, many are powered by solar panels, which collect energy from the sun. The panels turn the sunlight into power, which allows the robot to move and communicate.

CURIOSITY
ROVER

ROBOT COMPONENTS

Most robots share basic components, or parts. Sensors help the robot learn about its surroundings. Effectors, such as robotic arms, help the robot interact with its surroundings. Actuators are the motors that move the parts of a robot, such as the effectors. They may also move the parts that help the robot travel, such as wheels and treads. The controller is like the robot's brain. It guides the robot to perform a set of preprogrammed actions. Other robots are controlled remotely, or from a distance, by an operator.

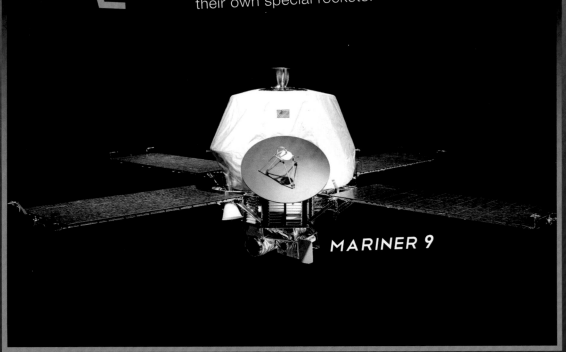

Some robots used on the ISS are brought aboard on space flights, but most robots working deeper in space are launched by their own special rockets.

MARINER 9

Robots communicate with scientists on Earth using antennas, or devices that send messages back to our planet. Many space robots, such as rovers, are actually controlled on Earth. Signals coming from operators on Earth tell the rovers what to do. These signals can take a long time to get from one antenna to another!

13

Some of the most important parts of space robots are their special sensors. These sensors gather data about the planets, moons, and asteroids they're studying. They analyze, or study closely, everything from surface soil to temperature. Special cameras take different kinds of photographs.

HUYGENS
PROBE

The *Cassini* orbiter was launched on October 15, 1997. It took around seven years to enter Saturn's orbit!

CASSINI ORBITER

Most of what we know about the planet Saturn, for example, comes from data robots have sent back to Earth. The orbiter *Cassini* became the first spacecraft to orbit Saturn on July 1, 2004. *Cassini* also carried a probe called *Huygens*, which used a parachute to land on Saturn's largest moon, Titan, in January 2005. *Cassini* and *Huygens* sent back data about Saturn, its moons, and the rings that circle the gas giant. *Cassini* used its sensors to gather data about Saturn.

CURIOUS ABOUT MARS

One of the most powerful rovers ever built is called *Curiosity*. Launched by NASA in 2011, it landed on Mars on August 6, 2012. The rover is about the size of a car. It's 10 feet (3 m) long, 9 feet (2.7 m) wide, and 7 feet (2.1 m) tall. It weighs 2,000 pounds (907.2 kg). *Curiosity* was designed to study the climate and geography of Mars. It also searches for signs of carbon, which is an element that's considered one of the building blocks of life.

Though *Curiosity's* mission was expected to last about two years, it's still used by NASA today to explore the "Red Planet." The six-wheeled rover is packed with sensors and equipment to help scientists learn more about Mars and its ability to host life in the past or present.

Curiosity has taught us a lot about Mars. Perhaps its biggest discovery so far has been that Mars could have supported **microbial** life in the past. This life may have been tiny and simple, but it's still important!

Unlike many robots in space, *Curiosity* doesn't need the sun for power. Its energy source is plutonium, an element that creates heat, which the robot turns into power. This lets *Curiosity* travel farther and for longer lengths of time than earlier Mars rovers such as *Spirit* and *Opportunity*.

This mast on the *Curiosity* rover includes sensors that measure the temperature and humidity of the planet. It's called the Rover Environmental Monitoring Station (REMS).

Curiosity has its own weather station on board, which keeps track of the wind speed, air pressure, **humidity**, and temperature on Mars's surface. It also has its own robotic arm, which is used to grab rock samples. Its chemistry lab can analyze these samples to learn information, which it sends back to Earth with its antenna. *Curiosity* even has a **laser** that can burn holes in rocks up to 23 feet (7 m) away!

FINDING WATER

Space robots have changed the way we think about planets in our solar system. Until recently, Earth was thought to be the only planet to have liquid water on its surface. Later, scientists thought Mars had liquid water on its surface at one time but that it was no longer present.

In 2015, *Curiosity* found liquid water just below the surface of Mars. Later that year, the *Mars **Reconnaissance Orbiter** (MRO)* discovered recent signs of flowing liquid water on Mars's surface. The *MRO* can't roam the surface like a rover, but it has six different tools to track potential water on the planet. It used a tool called an imaging **spectrometer** to track the trails left behind by water flowing on Mars's surface.

Scientists still think finding life on Mars is unlikely, but *Curiosity* and the *MRO* have changed the way we think about the planet.

THE HUBBLE TELESCOPE

You might not think a telescope is a robot, but it is when it's in space! Launched in 1990, the Hubble Space Telescope is one of the most advanced telescopes ever built. It uses solar panels to create energy. It stores some power in batteries for the 36 minutes it operates in Earth's shadow during its 97-minute orbit around our planet. Hubble was designed to survive big shifts in temperature. The temperature changes greatly during one orbit around Earth!

The telescope focuses its camera lens deep into space, sending hundreds of thousands of amazing photographs back to Earth. Hubble has studied **black holes** and other objects and **phenomena** deep in space. It's also helped scientists learn the age of our universe and find new planets far outside our solar system.

The telescope takes the data it receives and sends it through satellites to Goddard Space Flight Center in Maryland. Then, it receives new commands to turn the telescope toward a new subject deep in space.

HOW HUBBLE WORKS

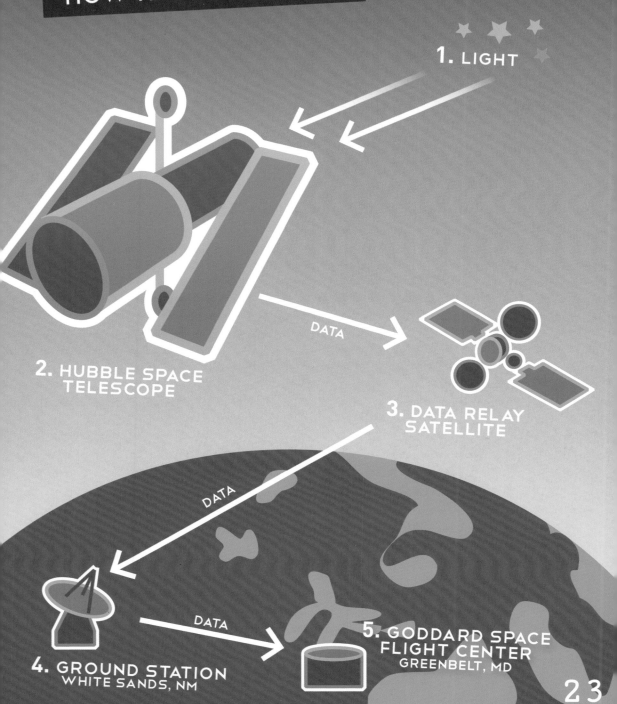

1. LIGHT

2. HUBBLE SPACE TELESCOPE

DATA

3. DATA RELAY SATELLITE

DATA

4. GROUND STATION
WHITE SANDS, NM

DATA

5. GODDARD SPACE FLIGHT CENTER
GREENBELT, MD

Robonaut is probably the closest thing NASA has to the walking, talking androids of science fiction. NASA began work on Robonaut in 1996. It has a head, upper body, arms, and hands just like a human. Robonaut's head has cameras that allow it to see. The robot works in two different ways: people give Robonaut a simple command to follow, or people use its cameras to see and then run the robot by remote control.

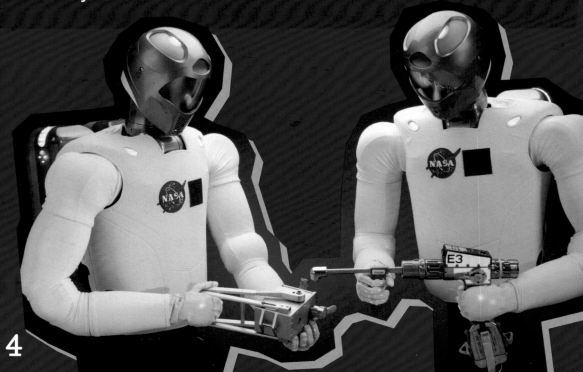

Robonaut 2 works in the Destiny laboratory
on the International Space Station.

Robonaut 2 works in the Destiny laboratory
on the International Space Station.

Robonaut 2 was first taken into space with a shuttle flight in 2011. Robonaut 2 is aboard the ISS and does simple tasks, such as flipping switches, so astronauts aboard the space station can focus on other tasks. NASA hopes future versions of Robonaut can take part in **spacewalks** and complete harder tasks.

LENDING A HAND

For the astronauts aboard the ISS, one of the most important space robots is an arm called Canadarm that can move large objects in space. The first Canadarm was used on the space shuttle in 1981. It was used to grab things outside the shuttle, such as the Hubble Space Telescope and other satellites.

Canadarm was made by the Canadian Space Agency.

DEXTRE WITH
CANADARM2

The ISS has a larger Canadarm2, which has been used to add new parts to the space station and even move astronauts around on spacewalks. The arm can be controlled by an astronaut aboard the ISS or even by someone back on Earth at mission control. People use a device called a **joystick** to control the robotic arm, moving it into place and grabbing things like a human hand could. The space station also has a smaller, humanlike hand called Dextre that can work with Canadarm2.

FUTURE ROBOTS

NASA is constantly testing new robots to help astronauts in space and scientists on Earth study the universe. One robot idea it's testing is called SPHERES. SPHERES are soccer-ball sized robots that have flown aboard the ISS since 2006. They are small satellites that are involved in many different experiments on the station. SPHERES have made breakthroughs in space research, and will continue to do so in the future.

Some engineers also hope a small robotic arm could be used inside the ISS in case of an emergency, such as an astronaut getting sick or hurt. If an astronaut needed surgery, for example, a doctor on Earth could take control of the arm and perform the surgery in Earth's orbit!

New robots are also being tested to explore new areas of space where people may one day travel.

From soccer ball-shaped robots to robotic arms, many different kinds of robots will help shape space research and travel in the future.

OUT OF THIS WORLD

In the future, robots will continue to aid research aboard space stations and push deeper into space. They'll take pictures and use special sensors to help us learn more about objects beyond Earth. Robots such as Valkyrie (Robonaut 5) may help NASA explore more locations too dangerous for humans to reach, allowing us to learn more about space and the limits of our technology in the ever-expanding universe.

Without robots, we wouldn't know much about space. They're important to our study of the universe, the safety of astronauts aboard the ISS, and future missions beyond Earth's orbit. From orbiters to rovers, space robots come in many different sizes and shapes and have special equipment to complete their tasks. Some robot missions are truly out of this world!

GLOSSARY

black hole: An invisible area in outer space with gravity so strong that light cannot get out of it.

humidity: The amount of moisture in the air.

International Space Station: A space station satellite that is occupied by astronauts from different countries. Many experiments and observations are made from this station.

interstellar: Having to do with the space between stars.

joystick: A control device that allows motion in two or more directions.

laser: A tool that uses a small, focused beam of light that can be used for many different tasks.

microbial: Relating to an extremely small living thing that can only be seen with a microscope.

phenomenon: A fact or event that is observed.

propulsion: A force that moves something forward.

reconnaissance: The exploration of a place to collect information.

satellite: An object that orbits another larger object.

spacewalk: The act of an astronaut moving around and doing work outside a spacecraft while it's in outer space.

spectrometer: A tool used to record and measure things in a

INDEX

WEBSITES

Due to the changing nature of Internet links, PowerKids Press has developed an online list of websites related to the subject of this book. This site is updated regularly. Please use this link to access the list: www.powerkidslinks.com/rar/space